SEWING PANTS FOR WOMEN

a guide to perfect fit

by ELSÉ TYROLER

published by
HEARTHSIDE PRESS, INC.
GREAT NECK, NEW YORK 11021

TABLE OF CONTENTS

PREFACE

Until World War II, pants were a man's prerogative, designed *for* men *by* men. Then Mother became an inventor of necessity. Off to defense plants she went, doffing aprons, donning pedal pushers, Capris, Bermudas, Jamaicas, and even short shorts. The clothing industry was caught with its preparedness down. Everyone, from patternmaker to manufacturer, took up the—sorry we must say it—slack, turning out women's pants by the only fitting methods they knew; men's tailoring. Results? Womanly curves were firmly entrenched in pants fit for men—and a new field of humor was created for the cartoonists.

As a specialist in fitting women's clothing, the pants picture was equally distressing to me. Good fit and modern lines: these were what women wanted, and these I set out to give them. By taking a fresh piece of paper, and by not borrowing any previous squiggles, I created a new concept of pants for women. The problem was not that women were not made for pants, but that pants were not made for women!

Here, on these pages, is the Elsé method of pants construction, just as I have taught it to my students and to members of the industry. Each step is developed logically and is accompanied by diagrams for each alteration.

The humor as well as the rollicking illustrations of women in Pantsville, U.S.A., are the contribution of Carolyn Keys. She has achieved the happy union of lightheartedness and a fine technical grasp of the subject. The effect will do much to cheer you on your way to an excellent fit in pants.

With compassion for your problems, and a few of the answers too, I remain . . .

ELSÉ

1

MAKE WAY FOR PANTS

Pants are here to stay. Most of us admitted that long ago. The only remaining question is: are they staying at the Ritz, or in some cold-water flat on the back streets of fashion?

Like country cousins moved to town, pants are beloved by all and their little idiosyncrasies are accepted as part of the package. What if they do have a few strange wrinkles in their personalities? What if their complete candor and utter frankness *is* a bit awkward in public? Pants are just plain folks. Besides, like country cousins, they are always good for a cartoon in the male humor mills!

Let's get our heads out of the sand, ladies! Pants have turned out to be rather important. They are worn for cocktails as well as gardening. They turn up in silks and satins under floating evening skirts. They stride forth on the golf course where they are expected to be as flawless as madame's game is not. They constitute the suburban uniform for the supermarket circuit.

Since they are so important, don't you think their fit needs as much attention as you give to suits and dresses? Pants, affording, as they do, so little opportunity for camouflage, should be tailored to your problems with exquisite care. Trousers of all sorts and shapes have become first-class citizens of fashion—and, as such, they should fit!

Of course they should. Everybody knows that, but only a few fortunate females can achieve this easily. Your chances for simply stepping into a pair of pants and cutting the sort of figure you see in your mind's eye are about as great as your chances for winning on a sweepstakes ticket. No matter what the measurements are on the stub, you are bound to differ at least a bit from the shape of the pants; enough to give a new twist to your whole appearance.

If you are a pattern-envelope size twelve whose measurements, incredibly, match those given on the back of the envelope (even the ones *not* given) we are not talking to you. You may make your pants like a ready-mix cake and wear them with confidence, but how many of us really belong in that category? There is a story about an ancient Greek of high degree. He must have had a complex about his figure, because he ordered a bed made to his exact dimensions. When overnight guests came, he required them each to try *his* bed for size. If they proved too long and hung over a bit, he accommodatingly had them cut off to fit. No one was permitted to be taller than he. He had a very small circle of friends, just as the patternmakers of today have a very small circle who fit *their* pants!

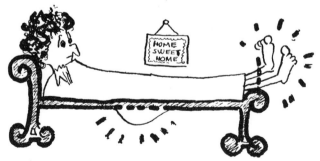

There are so many ways to go astray. So your waist, hips, and length of limb vary not one iota from the dimensions given on the back of a pattern envelope? What about your crotch length? Did you know it is perfectly possible to be five foot two and have a long crotch, or to be a splendid six feet and have a short crotch?

Think about this: suppose your hips are a respectable 36 inches? Are they wide, and are you as flat as a pancake fore and aft, or are they narrow with a pleasant rotundity in prow and stern? It is quite possible for both shapes to have the same hip measurement, but they can't both wear the same cut of pants!

These are just a few of the ways a woman's contours have of boobytrapping her complacent statement that she is a *perfect* size twelve, or sixteen, or twenty. There are so many different ways to be perfect! To inject a little realism into this picture; let's open the lid on Pandora's Box and bring out all the less-than-perfect figures. A figure that has squared off in battle with creeping calories will not be enhanced by a lot of little pulls and wrinkles which emphasize its problems. If your heart is young and gay and you are not yet ready to go to a wienie-bake in sprigged calico, wear pants—no matter what your shape, but wear them with built-in fit, and, therefore, with pride. Remember, if you don't do much for pants, the pants still can do their best for you!

2

KNOW THYSELF! THE MEASUREMENT CHART

If your trousers are to fit you, they must be designed to your precise measurements before you ever set scissors to cloth. The first task is to know thyself!

The measurement chart

This is your basis for a perfect pair of pants. It is where fit is born. Follow the instructions carefully, and note all your findings in the allotted space. As you proceed through the fitting steps you constantly will be referred back to this chart, so lay your foundation now with accuracy.

The old saw about the perfect 36-24-36 figure doesn't tell you a thing. One woman with these measurements may have boy-skinny hips and a total lack of *derriere*. Another has the abundant curves of womanhood. Some women have tummies as flat as boards but rather a caboose to the rear; others billow out in front and present a less undulating terrain behind. As we said, they may all be 36-24-36, but *vive la difference!* The bottom 36 can be angular, softly curved, all in one place, or evenly distributed. We cannot expect each type to fit the same pants pattern, bought solely by hip measurement. This is why we cannot urge you strongly enough to know thyself—and to put all the incriminating evidence on the measurement chart.

Use a good tape measure—preferably plastic coated, which will hang straight when unfolded. Fasten a length of tape around your waist, snugly but not uncomfortably. Now call in a good friend to take the measurements while you *relax* and keep an eagle eye on her accuracy.

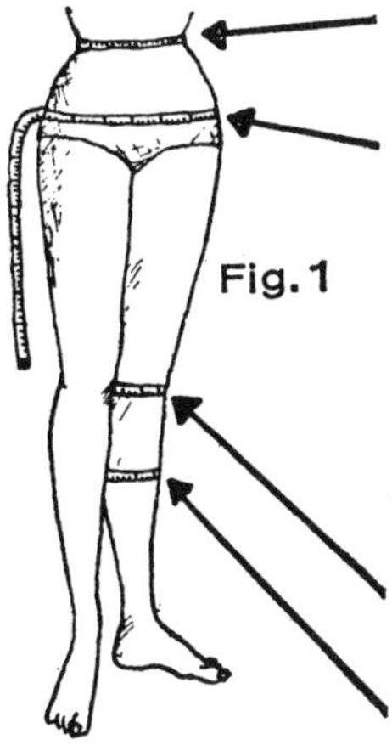

		INCHES
WAIST	Measure as firmly as you wear pants belt.	
HIPS	Place pins at 7″ or 8″ below waistline on both hips. Distance depends on body proportion. Measure around hips over pins.	
KNEE	Measure around knee.	
CALF	Measure around calf.	
INSTEP	Measure around instep.	
SIDE LENGTH TO KNEE	Measure from waist to center of knee.	
SIDE LENGTH TO ANKLE	Measure from waist to ankle bone or to desired length.	
CROTCH LENGTH	Sit on chair having flat seat (or on table). Measure from waist to top of chair seat (or table top).	

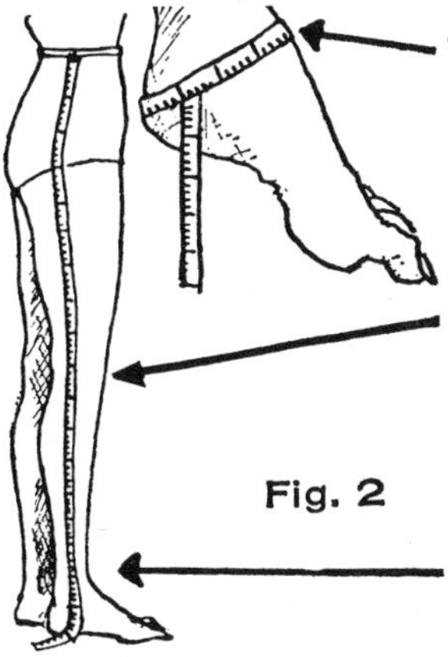

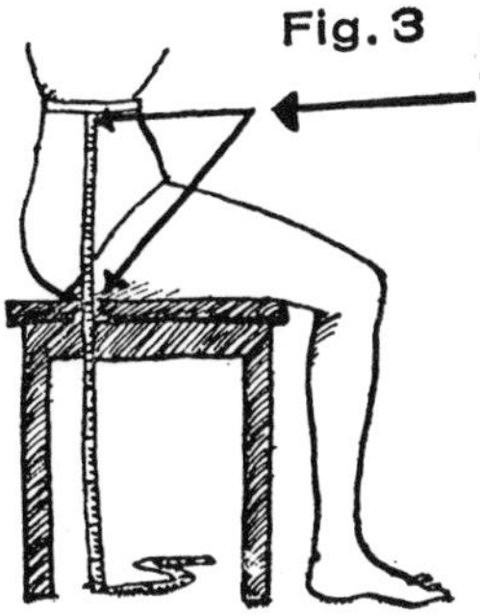

Fig. 1

Fig. 2

Fig. 3

3

TAKE SEVEN GIANT STEPS TO PANTS PERFECTION

Strangely enough, all that has ever been written about how to fit a pair of pants could be put in a thimble—and still leave room for your finger. In spite of the fact that they are undoubtedly the most demanding piece of apparel when it comes to fit, pants are the perennial stepchildren of the pattern instruction sheets.

Meticulous instructions are given for sewing the whole business together. And patternmakers do consider that women come in a variety of heights, but woe, oh woe, to the woman who earnestly constructs her pair of pants, only to find that the finished product goes *in* where she goes *out!* We think that you will find the following steps in making or altering pants far easier, in the long run, than extensive plastic surgery.

Step 1 Preparing the pattern for alteration

Your pattern is a blueprint for constructing a fine pair of pants. Is it a printed pattern? If it is, it probably has the hip, knee, and

hem line already drawn in. If it has not, get out your ruler and triangle and prepare to draw them in yourself, always measuring from
seam lines rather than cutting lines. Perhaps it will cure your artistic
jitters to take a look at Figure 4 which you will use for the following
alterations.

Take the vertical waist-to-hip measurement from the chart. On the
pattern, measure down that distance from the waist on both front and
back pieces, establishing points through which you will draw a horizontal line. This line, drawn parallel to the printed alteration line
and all the way across, will henceforth be called your hip line and
alteration line.

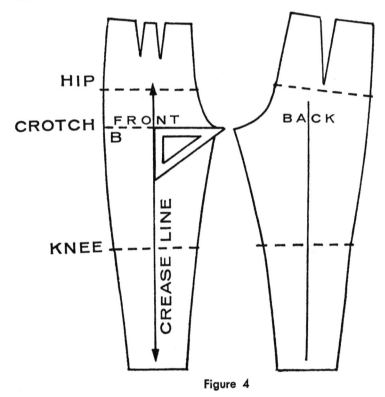

Figure 4

Locate the Crotch Length on your pattern Front by placing a triangle on the straight-of-goods in such a manner that it meets the point
of the crotch. See Figure 4. Draw a line across the top of the triangle
to "B" as indicated on the diagram.

Draw in the hem-line. Locate the knee-line, usually half the way
between the hem and the crotch, and carefully draw a horizontal line
at that point.

Draw a crease-line in center, both front and back. When you finish,
you should have a workmanlike pattern, drawn in the manner
illustrated.

Step 2   Length alterations: crotch, knee, and full side

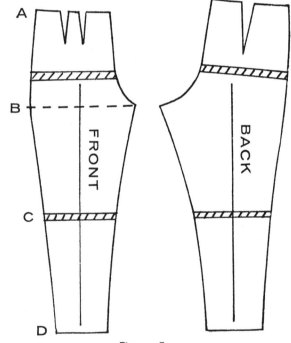

Figure 5

First we will deal with the crotch length. Take the Crotch Length from the measurement chart. Then, add to it the necessary *ease:*

For small sizes (hips below 35 inches) add ½ inch.

For medium sizes (hips 35 to 38 inches) add ¾ inch.

For large sizes (hips over 38 inches) add 1 inch.

For stretch fabrics, reduce the ease by half these amounts. For tight fitting pants, reduce the ease slightly, especially if the fabric has some give to it.

Let's correct the pattern itself. Look at Figure 5. Measure the length from *A* to *B* on your pattern. Compare this figure with your own crotch measurement *plus* the necessary amount of ease. If the pattern is too long, draw a parallel line below the hip-line and fold out the excess. Do the same in the back. If the pattern is too short compared to you, cut it along the hip line. Lengthen it by inserting the needed amount of extra paper *all the way across*, see Figure 5.

The knee length: Some women are long from ankle to knee, some are long from knee to hip. It couldn't matter less which you are, unless you have ambitions for the Folies Bergere, *or* unless you have a hankering for a pair of Bermudas, Jamaicas, house boy pants, pedal pushers or any type of pants whose length relies upon the knee!

So regard that knee-line you made in step one with suspicion, until you have determined whether it coincides with yours, or not.

Locate knee length: Refer to your knee length on the chart and apply it to your pattern. Measure the pattern from *A* to *C*. See Figure 5. If the measurements are the same, you're home safe. If not, draw a new, correct knee-line parallel to the existing knee-line (either above or below). Make the line with a red pencil so you'll know it's yours. This step is important when styling different lengths of pants.

The full side length: To adjust, compare your measurement from the chart with the length of pattern. If there is a discrepancy, shorten or lengthen the pattern *below* your knee-line. Make certain that you keep your lines parallel. Add or remove the same amount both in front and in back.

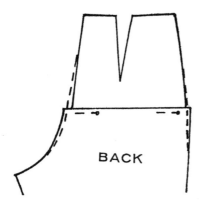

BACK

Figure 6

Seams that do not meet after alteration: Adjust your lines as shown in Figure 6 by the *broken line.* It is a matter of giving a little and taking a little to arrive at a compromise between the original lines.

Step 3   Hip alterations

There are as many different humps and bumps to a pair of pants as there are women to walk around in them. And there is certainly no area more susceptible to poor fit than the hips if you attempt to squeeze all those varied contours into one pattern shape. Might as well try to add apples and oranges. Or bananas and pears, for that matter!

On your measurement chart you have all the information you need to personalize a pattern so that it will fit you and your particular terrain.

Pin your Front and Back pattern pieces together by matching side seams at the hip-line. (Remember those two pins at the fullest point of your hips, about seven or eight inches down?) Take a look at Figure 7 to see what you should be doing.

Now comes a little arithmetic in two-part time: look up your hip measurement and add two inches to it for ease. This represents the total hip circumference you will need in your pattern, but remember

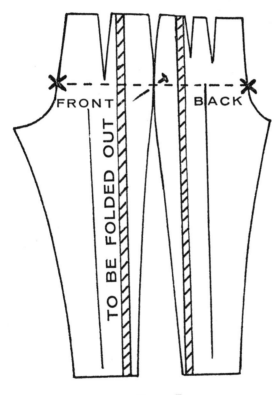

Figure 7

that the two pieces of your pattern represent only *half* your figure. So, the next operation will be to divide your total hip circumference by two—and you have the number of inches your pattern must measure to fit you.

Back to the pinned-together pattern. Measure from the center front (the X to the left of Figure 7) to the center back (the X on the right). If the measurement is more than the number of inches you determined in the preceding paragraph, you will take one-half the difference out of the pattern Front and one-half out of the Back, if you are fairly standard in front and back.

This alteration is made on a vertical line, designated by the alteration line on the diagram, so that it will not disturb the side seam curve. (Do not make the common mistake of adding only at the hips, because that will make the side seam ripple and cause great difficulty when it comes to inserting the zipper.) An example: if the pattern is 1 inch too large, fold out ½ inch in front and  ½ inch in back. Be sure to fold it out *all the way* from the waist to the hem, as shown in Figure 7. Similarly, if the pattern is too small by 1 inch, insert ½ inch of extra paper in the front and ½ inch in the back. You are now grading or sizing the pattern up or down a fraction of a size.

Remember your hip measurement is not all hip. It also includes the seat and abdomen. If your hips curve more than standard, add a little more at the side seams to take care of the excess. This is particularly necessary where the hips are prominent.

If you have very straight hips, the curve at the side seams must be decreased in front and in back. Be sure to decrease in equal amounts, however. See dotted lines, Figure 8.

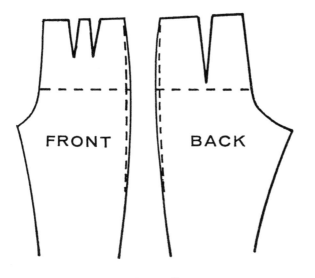

Figure 8

Always operate where your figure requires it. Sometimes you grade or size only in front—sometimes only in back. For example, you may need to add only a small amount to your hip measurement —let's say about ½ inch. If you protrude more in front over the abdomen than the standard figure, then insert only in front. Or perhaps your seat is standard plus—or on the prominent side. Then insert only through the back portion.

Do the same grading if you want to make the pattern smaller. For a figure with a flat abdomen, fold out a small amount in front only, or do the same in back for a flat seat.

After you have made any of these alterations, and have decreased or increased the width of your pattern pieces, remember to *draw a new crease-line* vertically through the exact center of the knee-line and parallel to the former crease-line. The reason for this is that when inserting or decreasing the pattern piece, the crease-line moves over half the amount of any change made.

Step 4   Hang of the pants at the waist and crotch *width* alterations

There is an old and weary joke about a person's legs being just long enough to reach the floor. It is also axiomatic that the shortest

distance between two points is a straight line. Now, suppose we start at the *waist* smack in the center of the back and envision two lines traveling to the floor. If the person involved has a very flat seat, the route from waist to floor *will* be a straight line. But if she also throws her hips forward making her tummy rather prominent, you can see that the line from waist to floor in front has to travel over the prominence en route; therefore it is not a straight line—*and* is longer than the line to the rear.

A similar situation develops if the subject has a bustle back and a flat stomach. In other words, it is possible for a pair of pants to be a different length from waist to floor in front and back. This is also true of a person who carries no extra weight, but simply tilts her hips forward or backward so that her waist line is at a slant. See Figures 9, 10, 11. These three figures each have the same hip measurements. Figure 9 shows a standard (or perhaps ideal!) shape. The anatomy is evenly balanced and requires little or no alteration. Figure 10 shows a shape which is wider through the seat. It is rounder in circumference through the hips, and is more like a true circle. This type requires a longer line in the back to reach from the waist to the floor as

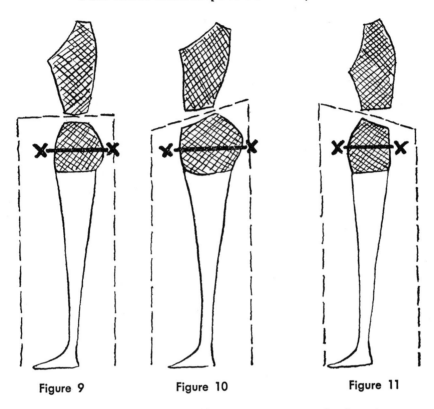

| Figure 9 | Figure 10 | Figure 11 |

shown in Figure 12. Add ¼ to ½ inch at the center back waist seam, tapering to nothing at the side seams.

Figure 11 is very flat in the seat. This type requires a far shorter line from waist to floor in the back. In this case, drop the waistline ¼ to ½ inch at the center back seam, tapering, as before, to nothing at the side seams. You will find this technique illustrated by the dotted line at the top of Figure 13.

Look again at Figure 10. Compare the distance between the X's on this type—this is called the *crotch width*—with the distance between the X's on the other figures. Wider, isn't it? In order to fit this type, the crotch curve must be widened by adding to the inner leg seam at both front and back. See Figure 12.

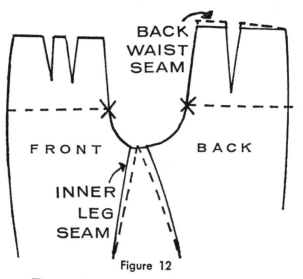

Figure 12

Look now at Figure 11. Judge the distance between the X's on this type. Her crotch width is narrower, isn't it? Therefore less crotch width is needed in the pattern, so the inner leg seam is decreased at the crotch by about ½ inch *in the back only*. This is shown by the

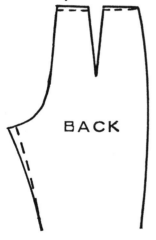

Figure 13

broken line at the side in Figure 13. It is sometimes necessary to alter this again after the first fitting. If it then proves to be still too wide, pin out a small amount at the *front* seam also.

Front alteration (the waistline seam): If your abdomen is flat, no alteration will be needed. However, if you tend to round out in front once the confining influence of a tight garment is removed, this is more apt to be a problem. If this is so, increase the center front by adding ¼ to ½ inch to the waistline, tapering to nothing at the side seams. See Figure 14.

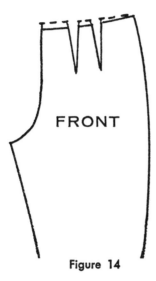

FRONT

Figure 14

Step 5   Waist and dart alterations

By manipulating the darts in a pattern you are molding your figure on paper, much as a sculptor does in clay. Is there a great difference between your waist and hips? Then it follows that *you* will need deeper darts, or more of them.

A curve on you requires a dart in the pattern. We cannot change your curves but we *can* change the darts to fit them. Study your figure in a mirror to assess what the measurement chart has told you, roll up your sleeves, and prepare to be-

Darts stop before
high point

come a sculptress on paper. Who knows? Your work of art may end up in a museum: *Woman, With Pin Holes.*

To adjust waist: Take your waist measurement and add 1 inch for ease. This is a very important one inch, for when it is properly eased onto your waistband it will eliminate all the unsightly wrinkles sometimes found below that area. When sewing, direct the ease to the places where the curves are more prominent, such as over the abdomen or above especially full hips. Otherwise, distribute the ease evenly, *except* between the seat darts where none at all is required.

To make the waist smaller: Study your figure. Do you have additional curves at the sides below the waist, often called a "shelf" or "pillow"? If you do, place an extra dart in the waistline of your pants. It can be located either in front or back, depending on the area of greatest need. This dart, usually about ½ inch deep and 2 inches long, is called a Baby Dart (one of the original Elsé fitting techniques), because of its small size. It is placed halfway between seat dart and side seam or front dart and side seam. See Figure 15. A slightly deeper and longer dart is used to fit a protruding hip bone at front, running down to meet the most prominent point of the hip.

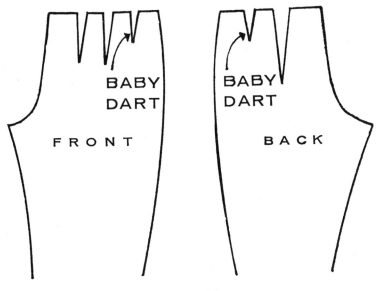

Figure 15

Depth and length of darts: Figure 16. The length and depth of darts can be changed to fit your individual figure. Always remember this about the *length* of darts: they must never run over the curve. Darts are used to provide fullness for a curve below. If they do not stop short of the fullest point, their purpose is defeated.

Look at Figure 16 and see how the back dart stops above the fullest part, indicated by the hip-line. It can stop at much as 2 or 3 inches above this point, depending on the need of your figure. Notice that it is also a much deeper dart than the front dart, indicating that the back curve is more prominent—a fact most of us admit!

The story for the front dart is quite different. The lesser curve of the abdomen requires that the dart be both shorter and shallower. But quite frequently the front dart and the back darts are pictured as being of equal length and depth! You will recognize this familiar problem. The long line of that front dart looks very striking in a sketch, but on your long-suffering person the effect is quite the opposite. If the dart is stitched down straight over the tummy (which rides rather high in most of us), the result is a dis- tressing pull and a fullness at the end of the dart. You may have had

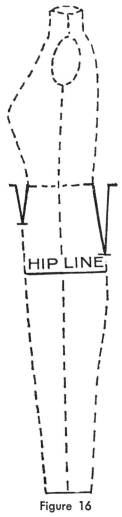

Figure 16

the same experience with a skirt, which, fitting too tightly across the tummy, puffed out below. The front dart is too long, and this is what to do about it!

In either a pattern or a finished garment, reduce both the length and the depth of the offending dart as shown by the broken line in

Figure 17. You may make one dart, if you need extra width to enlarge waist, or split it up into two smaller darts, as suits your fancy. The chart below will guide you in assessing the proper dimensions.

FRONT

Figure 17

Dimensions of Darts

Figure type		
Front (Abdomen)	*Depth*	*Length*
Flat	1 dart ½"	3"
Average	1 dart ⅝"	3-3½"
Average +	2 darts, each ⅝"	3-4"
Full	*1 baby dart ⅜-¾"	1¾-2½"
Back (Seat)		
Flat	1 dart ¾-1"	5-5½"
Average	1 dart 1¼"	5½-6"
Average +	2 dart, each 1"	5½-6"
Full	*1 baby dart ⅜-¾"	1¾-2½"

* Where there is an abundance of curves, two darts may be placed in front or in back.

Remember that your tape measure does not tell all. Use a mirror and a judicious eye to judge your type of figure and the darts required! You are working on a standard pattern or garment, so determine whether your figure is standard or on the plus or minus side in some places.

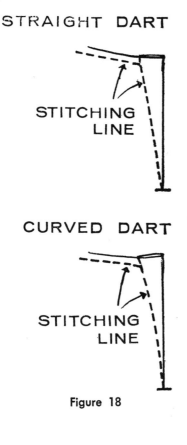

STRAIGHT DART

STITCHING LINE

CURVED DART

STITCHING LINE

Figure 18

Stitching darts: Figure 18. The proof of the pudding is in the eating. With darts, the proof is in the stitching. There is no hard and fast rule that says a dart must be straight! The majority of figures will fare quite well with straight darts, but if yours is an abundantly curved shape use *curved* darts. Remember this when setting needle to cloth.

Another point to remember, literally! Mark the ends of your darts with a horizontal line so that you will know when to stop stitching and will end up with darts of a uniform length. It doesn't matter whether you stitch from the waist down, or from the horizontal line up. Once you have placed your darts with the right depth and length, you may have a free hand in the rest of the operation and sew in either direction you choose!

Remember, in adjusting a waist, first adjust the darts for your abdomen and seat. Do not make the common mistake of operating on the side seams only.

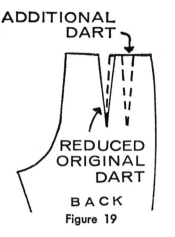

ADDITIONAL
DART

REDUCED
ORIGINAL
DART

B A C K

Figure 19

For a prominent seat: Figure 19. Since you have selected your pattern by hip-size (pants patterns should always be bought by hip measurement) an alteration for an overabundant seat is actually a reduction in the size of the waist in the back. Place a second dart 1 inch deep and 1 inch away from the existing one. Reduce original dart to 1 inch—see broken line in Figure 19.

Figure 20. If still further reduction is needed, take ¼ inch off at the center front seam, tapering down about 3 inches. The method is illustrated by the broken line. Do the same at the side seams on both front and back. No more than ¼ to ⅜ of an inch should be removed in this way.

To make the waist larger: First, adjust the darts. Make them shallower, or eliminate one dart altogether. For a particularly flat seat, decrease the seat dart to ¾ or 1 inch—then add at the side seams, front and back equally.

Perform the same operation for an unusually flat abdomen. In this case, you will need only one dart about ½ inch deep. If a still greater addition to the waist is needed, add it at the side seams, front and back equally. Always work through the darts first, then resort to the side seams if more alteration is needed.

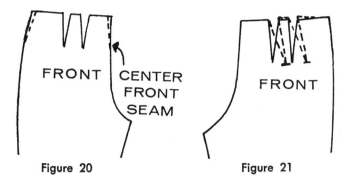

Figure 20   Figure 21

Diagonal darts: Figure 21. Diagonal darts may appeal to you as a style feature, or as a solution for prominent hip bones. In either case, change your darts to a slant-wise position. Either a flat abdomen or protruding hips—the two conditions often go together—can be fitted by swinging the darts to meet the nearest prominent projection. Darts are placed in your pattern to help you fit the complexities of your figure. You are not bound to use them as is; you are free to move them wherever they will do *you* the most good!

Step 6   Leg alterations

How tight should a pants leg be? A woman with particularly heavy thighs or heavy knees will be more comfortable and look more presentable in wider ones. A pleasing hem width would be one equal to the calf measurement. For a semi-tapered look use the calf measurement minus about 1 inch.

To widen a pants leg: Add an equal amount to both Front and Back at the hemline, continuing up

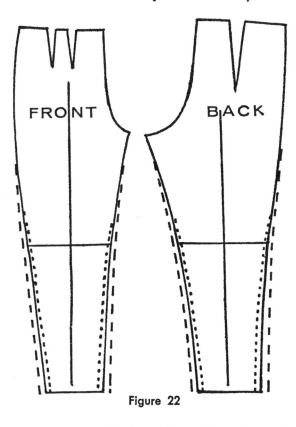

Figure 22

in the same manner past the knee line. Taper in to the lower hip line.

To attain the popular tapered look, first check your chart for your *instep* measurement. Your hem width must be at least as large as your instep, or you'll have a lovely pair of tapered pants you can't get into! Taper an equal amount on all four seams at the hem-line, blending into the seam-line and running slightly above the knee. For very slim legs, taper all the way to the crotch and hip line. See dotted line in Figure 22. Whenever you change the width of the legs, it must be done in *equal amounts on all four seams* to keep the crease line in the true center of the knee line.

Step 7   The back rise

What *is* the back rise, anyhow? When you look at the blueprint of a pair of pants, the back rise is your sitting room! It is the extra bit of length built into the center back seam to give you the necessary leeway for sitting, bending, and walking. No one can appreciate it more than the poor unfortunate who has heard that ominous rrrrrip in public!

Therefore, if you are intent upon constructing a pair of pants primarily for action—to wear for golf or bowling, or mountain climbing—you will want to be sure that they have the necessary back rise to make such abandon possible. By the same token, if you desire pure chic and fashion, the amount of back rise will determine whether they *do* hang arrow-straight from the seat. In either case, too much of a good thing is going to give you that dreary droop in the seat that has a way of making any pair of pants look tired.

Remember that you cannot always have comfort for activity *and* an extremely straight hang from seat to hem. More active sports usually call for Bermudas or pedal pushers, and a slight sag in the rear is not as noticeable in this length as it would be in the long, tapered pants.

Take your fabric into consideration too. A soft fabric with more give through the seat will require less rise. Woolens and unlined knit fabrics (or knits) need very little, and a stretch fabric needs no back rise at all.

It is difficult to determine just how much rise a pattern maker has built into his pattern. When you cut a pair of pants from a pattern be sure to *leave extra seam allowance*. That is, add 1 inch instead of the usual ⅝ inch to the center, waistline, and side seams in back. Add 1 inch allowance to front waistline seam *only*. See Figure 23. Broken line indicates seam allowance.

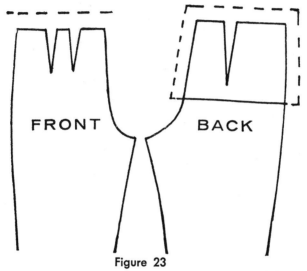

Figure 23

The dismal results of too much back rise is a seat that droops and hangs down like the tail of a whipped puppy. The fault cannot be corrected by taking it up at the waist, nor is it associated with the length of the crotch. If you find, at the first fitting of pants cut from a pattern, that this is the case (as in Figure 24), pin out the excess rise in a tuck across the seat at the hip line. Starting at center and pinning tuck along hip-line, taper to nothing at the side seam. You will transfer the same amount of tuck to the pattern by cutting the pattern

Figure 24

BACK

Figure 25

along the hip-line, from center back seam to side seam. Then overlap the lower half over the upper half at the center back seam and taper to nothing at the side seam. Reshape the crotch curve slightly, as shown by broken line in Figure 25. Also use these directions for alterations on ready-made pants.

Having now adjusted the pattern to the exact amount of rise needed by *you*, rip the side seams of your garment down far enough to permit re-placing the pattern upon it, and re-mark to the new dimensions. You see now why we warned you to leave a little extra seam allowance when cutting from a pattern for the first time.

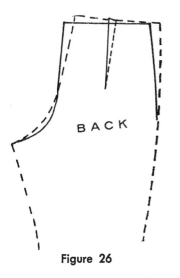

Figure 26

In altering a pair of ready-made pants for which you do not have a pattern, drop the waist the same amount that you pinned out across the seat at center. See Figure 26. The broken line is the former stitching line. The side and the center seam move over and assume a new position. See solid line.

How do you know how much back rise to eliminate? For long, glamorous pants that look their best when hanging in a die-straight line below the seat, a shorter back rise is required. Take out ½ to 1 inch by cutting the pattern from the center back seam along the hip-line to the side seam. Overlap the correct amount at the center, taper to nothing at side seam. Adjust the crotch curve as in Figure 25.

Pants intended for strenuous sports need more rise for movement. Cut across the hip-line from center back to side seam, and pin pattern to an insert about ½ inch wide at the center seam, tapering to nothing at the sides. Adjust the crotch curve as in Figure 27.

Modern pants need a deeper curve than patterns and ready-made

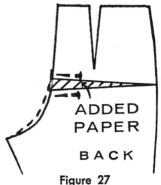

ADDED PAPER

BACK

Figure 27

pants allow. The curve must be deepened on the pattern or pinned in on ready-made pants. See Figure 25. For a cupped-in look, the curve must be fitted deeply, and a small amount tapered off the crotch point in back. See "Crotch Width Alterations," page 21. These alterations apply to the back ONLY. They will not work on the front.

4.

SEWING INSTRUCTIONS FOR PERFECT FIT

We assume that you have not set about the task of do-it-yourself pants without a pattern. Of course, your commercial pattern has its own set of sewing instructions. Don't get delusions of grandeur and toss them out the window! You will need to follow them precisely for all the little details that lend superficial style to your trousers. Pockets, belts, slits and loops—all the detailed how-tos of construction are executed according to your instruction sheet. The first thing to do is read over *both* the Elsé and the commercial instructions. Note where and when you will have to refer to the commercial pattern. Otherwise, follow the method set forth below.

The groundwork

Test your pattern in denim: Make your first pair of pants in an inexpensive cotton material such as denim. This pair is a trial run, subject to minor re-adjustment and trial-by-wearing. *Do not choose muslin for this purpose.* Using muslin makes fitting trousers more

36

difficult, and, besides, why not have pants worth wearing in public.

Cut your fabric with accuracy: There's many a slip twixt snip and fit, and what isn't there cannot be added. By the way, if you would like to achieve that very tapered look in pants, choose a fabric with give. It is a quality that can be determined by hand-to-hand test or found with certainty in a stretch fabric. Don't look for true taper in stiff and hard-finish cloth. It can't be done!

Transfer all markings carefully: Use a tracing wheel or make tailor tacks, and exercise a dogged devotion to accuracy. No room for impressionistic rendering, here! Pay special attention to marking the creaselines, being sure that your marks will be visible on the right side of the fabric as an easy guide to pressing. For best results make tailor tacks.

Choose your zipper location: This is a matter of personal taste. We assume that you chose your pattern with zipper site in mind. If not, barring interference with the style of the garment, the decision is now yours to make. As a general rule, a zipper placed either in front or back is preferable for full and rounded hips.

Do not stay stitch: If your instructions call for slavish stay stitching, ignore that part. You will find that the Elsé fitting instructions require occasional stretching and easing of the fabric. Stay stitching will only hamper you by its inflexibility.

Preliminary pressing: This is an important step that comes before you sew a stitch, so turn to the pressing section on page 57.

The actual sewing

1. Center back: Figure 28. Stitch darts. Seam back center together (leaving an opening for the zipper, if desired) stopping at the lower curve about 1 inch short of the leg seam. Stretch the seam

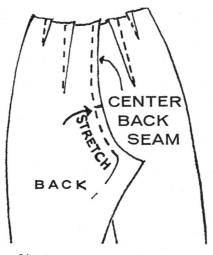

Figure 28

about ½ to ¾ of an inch, depending on give of fabric through the lower curve *in back only,* when stitching and pressing. This stretching will not only mold fit right into your pants, it will also prevent split seams at this point of great tension.

2. *Center front:* Figure 29. Stitch darts. Seam front center down to about 1 inch from leg seam.

3. *Leg seams:* Stitch inner leg seams. Stitch outer leg seams, leaving

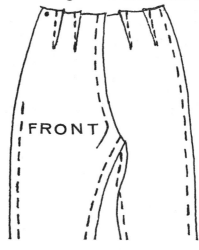

Figure 29

an opening for the zipper if not already provided for in back. Press seams open. See Chapter 8 on pressing.

4. *Curved seams:* Figure 30. Finish curved (crotch) seams. Reinforce by stitching again from start to finish of the curve. Clip the inner curve to ¼ inch of remaining seam, both back and front. These clips, should be about 2 inches below the hip-line. Press front and back seams open from waist to clipping. Curved seam between the clips is *not* pressed open, but is trimmed down to ⅜ inch.

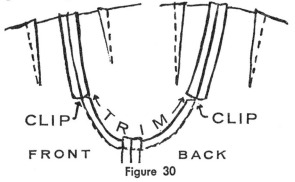

Figure 30

5. *The zipper:* In preparing the pants for a first fitting, you may simply baste under one side of the closing and mark the other side with a colored basting thread for an accurate pinned closing or place the zipper.

6. *The waist:* Ease waist on to waistband. There should be about 1 inch of ease in the waist seam to be eased on to either waistband or facing, to prevent any drawing or pulling below the waist. If you are using a fabric that does not shrink readily, stitch seams or darts slightly deeper at the waist. Do not ease through center back between the seat darts. Direct the ease evenly to all other areas, or concentrate it more where curves are more pronounced. Close with buttonhole or hooks and eyes.

7. *Hems:* TURN UP HEMS.

8. *Pressing:* Press crease in front to just below darts. Do same in back, stopping at crotch length. Follow crease markings in both.

5

THE DRESS REHEARSAL—FIRST FITTING!

If you have faithfully learned the lines of Seven Giant Steps to Pants Perfection, your anguish should be at a minimum. However, even the best of all possible plays has a few awkward bits of stage business that show up in a dress rehearsal. In our case, little individual body quirks you didn't know you had may become apparent. Take heart, and as does the playwright who must rewrite his lines, you must remember to take any little oddity back to your pattern and make the changes there as well as in the finished product.

Now for the fitting: Be sure you have sewn a belt onto the waist, or that you at least have a band basted to it. Pants hang from the waist. Don't try hold them up with your hands and achieve fit at the same time!

The closing should be basted under on one side and the other marked with colored basting stitches for an accurate pinned closing. If you are quite hippy put zipper in front or back, otherwise at any place you wish.

1. Check the waist band for comfort, letting it out or in as needed. This will affect the darts, making them deeper or shallower at the right place, either front or back.

2. Check hip comfort, letting in or out slightly at side seams.

3. Check crotch length. Does it hang too low? Then pin an even tuck all around the hip-line. Is the crotch too short? Go back to Step 2, page 14 for the alteration. If it is only a matter of ¼ to ½ inch, drop the waistline that amount.

4. Check the crotch width. Are you comfortable? Is there a pull across front or back at the crotch point level? Then let out the seams on the inner legs at the crotch point. (See Step 4, page 20.) Perhaps there is too much leeway in this area. Take the seams in, especially if you covet that cupped-in look of the younger generation. In this case, taper a sharper inward curve down to the knee line.

5. Check the back rise. If any droopiness has crept in, or the seat does not hang as straight as you would have it, pin out a tuck across the seat. (See Step 1, page 12.)
   If your pants pull in the center when bending or sitting:
   a. Look at the waist center, front and back. There may be too much dip or drop. If this is so, set the waistband higher, tapering to nothing at the sides.
   b. If more rise is needed, alter pattern by opening at center back about ½ an inch and re-mark pants with altered pattern.

6. Check for leg comfort. This is a matter of taste as well as fit. Take in or let out seams by the same technique you learned in Step 6, (page 30). Be sure to keep the crease-line in the center!

The pants with a smile

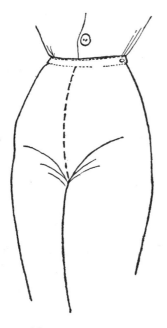

A smile is a very pleasant thing indeed, except when it refers to wrinkles in the front of your pants! Among the familiars of the garment trade, "pants that smile in front" is the euphemistic term used to describe garments with wrinkles that flair upwards from the crotch, as shown in the illustration. And it is nothing to grin about!

The cause is varied: there may be insufficient crotch width. In this case the malady can be cured by referring back to Crotch Width Alterations on page 21. There you will find instructions for widening this area. Often, wrinkles are caused by too snug a fit through the hip at the side seams. Misjudged hips or heavy thighs may need more breathing space. Release the side seams and see if that doesn't do away with the *unwanted* smile.

To cup or not to cup—that is the question!

The cupped-in look is a modern trend among the young-at-heart. See the illustration. Perhaps you admire it, perhaps you don't. There are followers for both schools of thought.

This contour fit is achieved by reducing the crotch points *in back only,* and by deepening the seat curve. The crotch curve must be a straighter, downward-plunging line with a sharp turn inwards. See Figure 31.

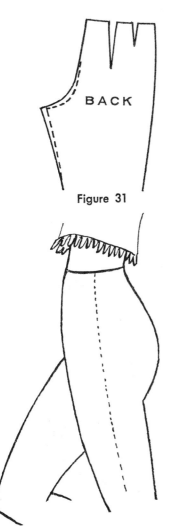

BACK

Figure 31

Perhaps you are not devoted to the cupped look, but find that there is simply too much fullness across or just below the seat. Making the crotch curve a straighter, downward-plunging line or giving it a sharp turn inwards (or both) will serve to remedy the situation.

If any of these last-minute changes have cropped up in your fitting, and you have conscientiously made the changes in your pattern, you can go forth knowing that you are now the proud possessor of a true-blue pants pattern that is yours, all *yours!* The final sweet reward will come when you sit back and dream of the rows upon rows of perfect pants that are yours for the making!

6

THE THREE-HEADED DRAGON OF PANTS CONSTRUCTION

With your trusty needle for a lance, you must slay this awesome dragon! Use this chapter for a shield! Know why pants sag and bag and won't sit down and half the battle is won. The other half can simply be avoided.

Baggy pants

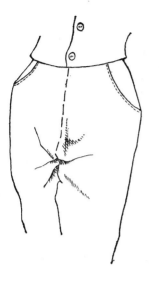

Pants were originally designed for men, by men. In attempting to fit them to milady's more diminutive waist and rococo hips, the patternmakers applied what knowledge they had—all of which had worked for men—and what usually happened? This! Pants that bagged in front! The center front seam took off like a ski jump—bias all the way! Figure 32 illustrates such a seam in action. Its only possible use is to fit the figure beside it! Pants hang from the waist, just like a slim, tailored skirt. Try taking a straight skirt pattern and changing the center front seam to a bias. What happens? The skirt would pouch out in front like a cow-catcher, wouldn't it? That is exactly what pants do when their center front seam is bias-cut. The evidence appears as baggy wrinkles across the crotch. The fault lies in the design of the pattern itself; there is no cure for it. If you already own such a pair of pants, save them for the next fashionable garage-cleaning you are invited to—and look for another brand of pants.

Pants that sag in back

The same principle holds true here. If the center *back* seam is cut on a *distinct bias*—and you are not—you are in for a bad case of the sags! (See Figure 33.) It is *not* a question of too much length in the back seat seam. It cannot be cured by "taking a little tuck across the

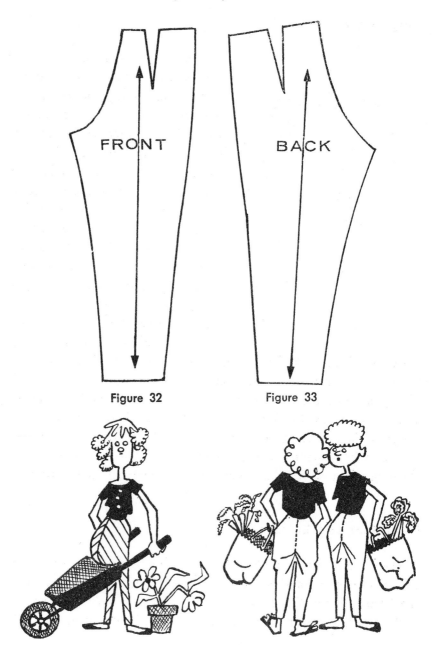

Figure 32   Figure 33

FRONT   BACK

seat." Such a remedy would be about as effective as giving aspirin to a drowning man; it is not a nagging headache he is bothered with, but a whole way of life. So it is with a bias-cut seat seam. Alter, adjust, take tucks, let in, and let out all you want, but nothing is going to change the basic situation. A bias-cut seat seam sags because it *is* bias-cut, and there is nothing you can do about it. If you are the chagrined owner of pants of this description, throw a coat on over them and dash out for another pair.

Pants that won't sit down

Perhaps you know the ones we are talking about. When *you* sit down, *they* pull down in back. The effect ranges all the way from discomfort when sitting to a general public announcement of what you wear beneath those back-sliding pants.

What to do about it? Well, you can always balance yourself on the end of your spine, like a board propped in the corner, for there is no handy relief for your distress. The fault again is in the construction of the pattern: that old devil, bias back seam, is with us again.

Think of it this way. Picture the seat curve of your pattern as a contour chair. Could you sit in it comfortably, with suitably erect posture, in no danger of sliding off?

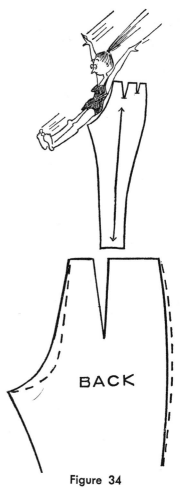

In Figure 34, the broken line represents the back center seam of a pair of pants with sitting room; the solid line shows a bias seam guaranteed to keep you in misery for the life of the pants. The distance between the two is your margin for composed sitting. The solid-line bias seam, forced to conform to the dotted-line straight seam when you sit down, pulls your pants down in back exactly the distance between the two. Look for pants construction with a seat seam shaped like the dotted line, or put

Figure 34

the shape in as shown in Figure 34. You will most likely have to add to the side seams.

Recognizing a well-constructed pattern

Now that you know all about the wrong sort of construction, just what do you look for to assure no-bag, no-sag, sitting-down pants?

A good pattern has a fairly straight up-and-down center seam in both front and back. Remember that pants hang from the waist just like a slim, tailored skirt. The center seams must be straight or the skirt will flare: the center seams of pants must be straight or they will bag. There will be a tiny bit of bias to a well-constructed pattern, just enough to accommodate the human figure, but never enough to condemn you to eternal bagginess, sagginess, and miserable sitting. You should be able to sit on that seat curve without sliding off!

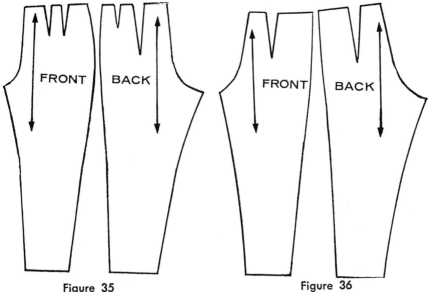

Figure 35   Figure 36

Compare Figure 35 and Figure 36. In Figure 35 you see a well-constructed pattern. See how the hips curve to accommodate a woman's shape. Notice that the *center seams* are virtually straight up and down. In the poor construction in Figure 36 the *side seams* at the hip-line are quite straight—and the center seams are cut on the bias. Here is what happened; the curve was taken off the hips and put in the center crotch seams. There is probably the same amount of room in the two patterns, but it is in the wrong place! The Good Lord put your hips where they are—and that is where the curve must be.

7

ADDING STYLE TO A BASIC PATTERN

A basic pattern is *you* on paper. It is made or altered to your measure, faithful to your every contour and lacking any nagging need for alteration. When it has been perfected you are free to design at will. For a good basic pattern is just this; a splendid *fitting tool* from which to create any variety of pants you fancy. If your basic pattern is designed to fit well, it will carry whatever style you ask of it. If, on the other hand, you add style to faulty fit, you are only adding insult to injury. First, be sure of your fit. Then choose whatever style you prefer.

Style is a spice *added* to fit according to taste. It may be the length of your pants, the width of your pants, even the pockets of your pants. To some minds it is a perky little bow perched on one prominence or another. There is one thing style is not: it is not a magic wand to transform poor fit into high fashion.

Tapered pants

If you have a yen for slinky pants with next-to-nothing legs, refer back to Step 6 of the Seven Steps To Pants Perfection on page 30.

The diagram and instructions you will find there deal with leg width. Be sure to taper all four seams, as the directions read, and by all means don't get so carried away with tapering that you forget to leave instep-room to get your foot through! This necessity can become a style detail in itself, by finishing the outside seams in a jaunty little slit at the hem.

Bell bottoms

If you take a second startled look and find that current fashion is busy flirting with a pronounced flare at the hem-line, this, too, can be achieved from your basic pattern. Simply go back to Step 6, page 30, and add about 3 inches to all four seams at the hem-line, tapering to nothing at the knee-line. It is even smarter-looking, if you have slim knees, to make a pinch of ¼ to ½ inch at the kneeline, as shown in Figure 37.

Long or short?

The choice is yours from infinite variety. Work with a semi-tapered sloper, that is, a basic pattern which has been conservatively tapered in the manner described.

Figure 38. Draw a crotch line on the Front, as in Step 1, page 13. Do the same on the Back. Check to make sure that your side seams are the same length.

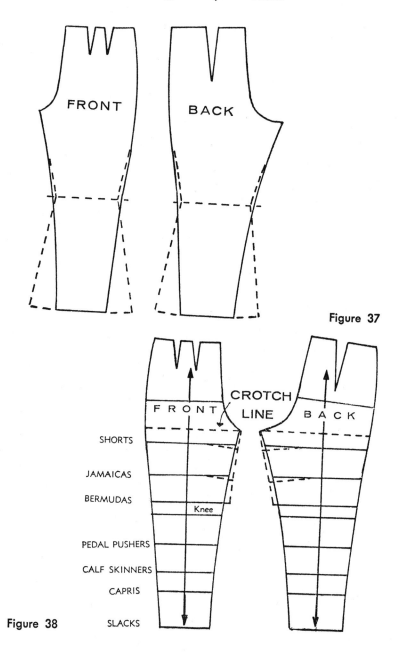

FRONT

BACK

Figure 37

CROTCH
LINE

FRONT

BACK

SHORTS

JAMAICAS

BERMUDAS

Knee

PEDAL PUSHERS

CALF SKINNERS

CAPRIS

Figure 38

SLACKS

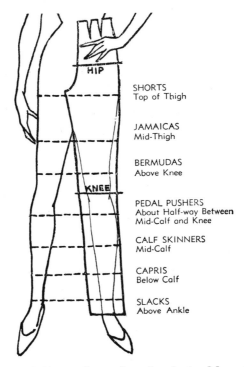

HIP

SHORTS
Top of Thigh

JAMAICAS
Mid-Thigh

BERMUDAS
Above Knee

KNEE

PEDAL PUSHERS
About Half-way Between
Mid-Calf and Knee

CALF SKINNERS
Mid-Calf

CAPRIS
Below Calf

SLACKS
Above Ankle

Figure 39

For shorts, Jamaicas, and Bermudas, select the desired length from Figure 39 and measure an equal distance down from the crotch line. Add about ½ inch to inner seams, front and back, and a lesser amount at the outer seams. Drop the hemline approximately ½ inch at the inner leg seam. Both these maneuvers are illustrated in Figure 38. You will find that dropping the hemline in such a manner takes care of the small kink at the inner leg seam so often seen in shorts. (This is sometimes seen in other lengths of pants, too, and can be corrected by smoothing out the inner and outer leg seams as you baste under the hem.)

For pedal pushers, calf skinners, Capris and any as-yet unborn whim of fashion, use the knee-line as your guide, measuring up or down the appropriate distance, and proceed in the same manner. It may be easier to use the hem-line as a guide for longer pants.

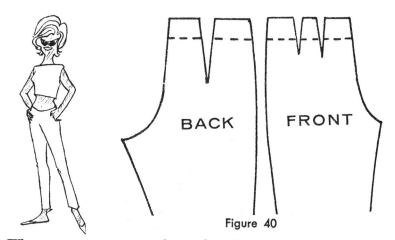

BACK   FRONT

Figure 40

Whatever name you give them—hipslingers, hiphuggers, hipriders —the weight of public opinion appears to be solidly behind them! The trend started on the French Riviera, crossed the Atlantic, and was influenced by the All-American blue jean. If you have both the inclination and the figure for them, they can easily be styled from your basic pattern.

As in Figure 40, measure down from waistline 2-2½ inches and draw a line following the original waist. This line will be your *finished* seam line for pants with a facing inside or outside. Add seam allowance when cutting away the top. If you prefer a waistband on your hipslingers, drop the seam line still lower, depending on the width of the proposed band. If you wonder what to do with the little leftovers of darts, particularly in front, don't stitch them, but ease on to facing or belting.

Tapered pants without side seams

Abandon hips, all ye who enter here! Pants without side seams are sleek, smooth, and smack of expensive price tags, but they are feasible only for the slim-hipped few, and recommended for smaller sizes. Any womanly swell about the hips, prominence in the thigh, or comfortable little billows below the hipline demand the presence of side seams to facilitate fit. It is one of the bitter truths of life that pants without side seams look dashingly alluring on models, but without a model's figure the picture is different. Be honest with yourself, and with your appearance. If you fill the bill, slim hips, no protrusions anywhere below the hipline, go to it! These pants can flatter your diminuendo figure lovingly. If you don't fill the bill, or fill it too amply, beware!

These pants are also made from a basic pattern. (See Figure 41.) Pin Front and Back together, 7 inches down, from the waist, matching side seams at hip-line. Try to overlap the side seams about ⅛ to ¼ inches. (This is what is meant by a closer fit!) Match the side seams at the hem-line, also.

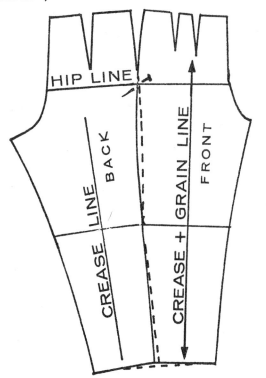

Figure 41

Now that you have matched the hem-line seams, take a look at the side seams below the hip-line. If they do not overlap more than a ½ inch, you are a candidate for this style of pants. If the overlap is greater, this is the point to abandon your plans and settle for pants with side seams!

You will find that some patterns cut for a pronounced tapered leg present an additional problem when used without side seams. When pinned together at hip-line and hem-line, the knee-line does not come together, adding extra width in this area. To correct this situation, overlap the side seams at the hemline ¼ to ½ inch. Be certain, in doing so, that you have left enough hem-line width to accommodate your instep measurement, unless you are fashioning a slit at the side or center front.

Adjust the hem-line, as shown by the broken line in Figure 41. Notice that the side seams at the waist now form a dart, which should end about 1 or 2 inches above the hip-line. The closing for this style of pants will be either in front or in back, according to your preference.

The grain and crease line will remain the same in the front. However, you will find the grain line in back will swing off. Don't worry about it. The original crease lines are still valid, and that is your only concern.

8

PRESSING YOUR PANTS

To some, pressing pants is as frustrating as a wrestling match with an octopus. To others, it is a simple business involving nothing more mysterious than straight lines. Neither is the case.

You will discover it is easy to set the creases in the Fronts before you have sewn a single seam! With the pants in this completely raw state, there are no distractions from either the crotch or back. Simply fold a Front precisely on its crease line (which, of course, you have dutifully marked with tailor's tacks in the cutting-out stage), making certain that the fold points squarely to the dart. As you press, remember that the front crease *stops just below the waist dart.* Later, you will see that a previously set front crease is a handy guide when setting the back crease.

Setting a crease

Is not a matter of making a few desultory passes with a steam iron —not if you would like a lasting and professional crease. The tools of the trade are few and simple. Your ironing board should have firm padding and not too much of it. Thick, soft padding may sound luxurious, but it will offer no resistance to your iron; a hard surface is essential to a knife-sharp crease. A steam iron is the most practical way of providing moisture, but on some fabrics it will raise a shine, so add a pressing cloth to your list. A striker is also needed. It is a

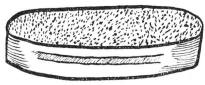

wooden instrument shaped somewhat like an iron and is used to strike or pound the steam into the fabric. If you don't own one, can't find one, or merely decline to make the purchase, you can use the bottom of your sleeve board with adequate results.

With these tools at hand, lay out the Fronts on the board with the fold on the crease line and pointing to the waist dart. Apply steam. Now, with the striker, pound the steam into the fabric until all the

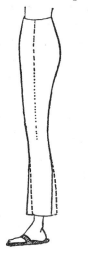

moisture has been absorbed.

Hold that iron! Before you step back to admire your handiwork and congratulate yourself on creases so straight that they make an arrow look like a wiggle-worm, think a minute. Are your *legs* as straight as that? Not if you walk around on them. You have a gentle swell to the calf muscle which is functionally necessary and cosmetically nice. Therefore, when you slip a leg into those arrow-straight pants, the sym-

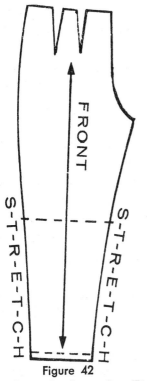

Figure 42

metry will be disturbed by that rounded calf. The fronts will be pulled toward the rear and their hems laid smack up against your shins as if you were standing in a gale. As the pants pull backwards to accommodate the shape of the calf, there is often a fringe benefit in the form of baggy knees. All the precision of your careful crease will be gone! And what can be done about it?

The cure for shin-plastered pants and baggy knees is part of pressing technique. After you have set the creases in the above manner, keep the pants on the board. Starting about 3 inches above the knee-line, stretch the side and inner leg seams of the Fronts, stopping about 3 inches above the hem. See Figure 42. As you stretch the two seams together, swing them forward until you have created a concave curve in the Front crease. The method is demonstrated in Figure 43. Con-

I'm the law, here, m'am

tinue stretching until you have added from ¼ to no more than ½ inch to the length, the amount depending on the give inherent in your fabric. When you have stretched the proper fraction of an inch, trim a corresponding amount off the Front hems, *the same amount all the way across.* In other words, if you have stretched ½ inch, *remove* ½ inch

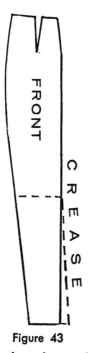

Figure 43

evenly from the Front hems. See Figure 42, broken line.

When you stitch the Fronts and Backs together along this stretched seam, the shape will hold. The slight concave curve of the crease will forestall the tendency to baggy knees, for it moves out away from your shins, distributing the hem width evenly, front and back.

Fabrics with give (especially stretch fabrics) need not be stretched in advance by pressing, but can be stretched directly at the machine. This is done when seams are joined and front seam is stretched to meet the longer back seam.

What about baggy knees in finished pants? The same procedure will work in this case, too. Rip the side seams to 3 inches above the knee-line. Stretch both inner and outer side seams of fronts only. When you have gained about ½ inch, you will see that you have achieved the typical concave curve in the crease line. Remove a like amount *evenly* all the way across the *Front* hems. Sew up the seams again and bid adieu to bags at the knees!

These things accomplished, your initial pressing chores are at an end. Press your seams as you go, paying special attention to the crotch curve. Remember that in this case, you press the front and back seams *open* from the waist down to the notches, but below that, through the crotch curve, you *do not* press the seams open at all. You will find further information when you return to the Sewing Instructions.

When the pants are finished, set the back creases with the striker, just as you did in front. Use the previously set front creases as a guide in laying out the pants. Back creases stop at crotch length. There! They look almost too impeccable to put on!

Don't hang up those pants!

Yes, of course, you were taught as a very small child to always say "please" and "thank you" and to always hang up your clothes. Quite commendable. But when you have just finished pressing a pair of pants, lay them on a flat surface for a period of time to allow the fabric to dry out thoroughly. All your preciously won concave curves may hang right out if you hang them up too soon! This procedure should be followed both with your unfinished front pieces and with freshly laundered finished pants.

CONCLUSION

Now we have come to the end of a perfect way. The ghosts of ancient pants problems have been laid to rest. No longer can the specters of men's alterations haunt the tailoring of women's pants.

On these pages you have found a concept of fit designed from its inception for women. Its impact will sweep the last vestige of cobwebs from your pants construction, and put you in the vanguard of an army of faultlessly fitted women in pants.

Now that pants have been made for women, it is triumphantly clear that women *were* made for pants!

THE END

INDEX